STONE COLD

#7 STONE COLD

GREG FARSHTEY – Writer
JOLYON YATES – Artist
LAURIE E. SMITH – Colourist

LEGO® NINJAGO™ Masters of Spinjitzu
Volume Seven: Stone Cold

Greg Farshtey – Writer
Joylon Yates– Artist
Laurie E. Smith – Colourist
Bryan Senka – Letterer

Published by Titan Comics, a division of Titan Publishing Group Ltd., 144 Southwark St., London, SE1 0UP. LEGO NINJAGO: VOLUME #7: STONE COLD.

A CIP catalogue record for this title is available from the British Library.

Printed in China.

First published in the USA and Canada in May 2013 by Papercutz.

10 9 8 7 6 5 4 3 2 1

ISBN: 9781782761983

www.titan-comics.com

www.LEGO.com

MEET THE MASTERS OF SPINJITZU...

LEGO
NINJAGO
Masters of Spinjitzu

And the Master of the Masters of Spinjitzu...

SENSEI WU

It hasn't been a very good day for the Ninja...
WHOA--
WHOA--
WHOA!
With Ninjago under attack by ancient stone warriors, the Ninja decided to try to take on these powerful foes...
OOOF!
It hasn't gone so well.
OUCH.
In fact, it's been about the worst defeat these four have ever suffered.
HOW... HUMILIATING.
At the end of the day, the Ninja drag themselves back to camp to report another failure to Sensei Wu...

WE DID OUR BEST. WE EACH CHALLENGED A STONE WARRIOR...
AND WE GOT OUR ROBES KICKED!
I USED ALL MY SKILLS AND TRAINING, AND YET I COULD NOT HARM MY OPPONENT.

FOUR TRIES, FOUR FLOPS. LET'S FACE IT, WE'RE JUST **LOSERS!**
NO. YOU ARE MERELY PROUD NINJA WARRIORS, FACING A TRUTH THAT ALL HEROES MUST FACE AT SOME TIME.

WHAT TRUTH IS THAT, SENSEI!?

I BELIEVE THERE IS A TALE THAT MUST NOW BE SHARED, BUT FIRST... YOU MUST KNOW THAT I ***LIED*** TO YOU ALL.

WHAT?
LIED TO US? HOW? WHEN?

YOU RECALL HOW I CAME TO EACH OF YOU TO RECRUIT YOU INTO MY NINJA TEAM.
DO YOU REMEMBER WHAT I SAID AT THE TIME?

I SENSE THAT THE TERRIBLE **LORD GARMADON** IS PLANNING TO RETURN TO NINJAGO. I NEED BRAVE NINJA TO STOP HIM.

SURE, I REMEMBER THAT. AND WE ALL JOINED UP AND WE BEAT GARMADON, OR STOPPED HIM, ANYHOW.

WHAT I SAID WAS ONLY HALF OF THE TRUTH... THERE WAS ANOTHER REASON I ASSEMBLED THIS TEAM.
NOW IT IS TIME YOU KNEW **THE TRUTH.**

"BEYOND THE EDGE OF THE WORLD," THE SENSEI BEGINS, "THERE IS A PLACE CALLED THE TOWER OF TEARS.
"IT HAS NO DOORS OR WINDOWS... ONLY A TRUE SPINJITZU MASTER KNOWS HOW TO GET IN OR OUT."
"IMPRISONED INSIDE THE TOWER WERE THE WORST VILLAINS ON THE PLANET... OR RATHER, THEY WERE IMPRISONED THERE UNTIL SOMEONE BLEW IT UP."
KA-BLAMM
"WITH THEIR PRISON DESTROYED, THEY WERE FREE TO STALK THE NIGHT AGAIN."
"AND TO SEEK REVENGE ON THE MAN WHO PUT THEM INTO THAT TOWER: SENSEI WU."

What is red and blue, covered in feathers, and very, very dangerous?

HMMMMM... THAT'S **EASY**...

"MY OLD FOE, KIRCHONN THE INVINCIBLE!"
FREE AT LAST!
NOW I CARVE OUT A NEW EMPIRE, BEGINNING RIGHT HERE!

"KIRCHONN ONCE LED A HORDE OF SIX-ARMED WARRIORS, UNTIL I TRAPPED THEM IN THE MOUNT OF SHADOWS."
"BUT EVEN ALONE, HE WAS A DANGER-- "

YOU MAY HAVE LOTS OF ARMS, BUT ONLY TWO FEET--
AND THEY ARE NO USE IF NOT ON THE GROUND!
SENSEI WU-- UNNGHH!

I WAS TOLD TO EXPECT YOU.
NOW I HAVE MY REVENGE!

NOT TODAY-- AND NOT UNARMED, AS YOU NOW ARE.

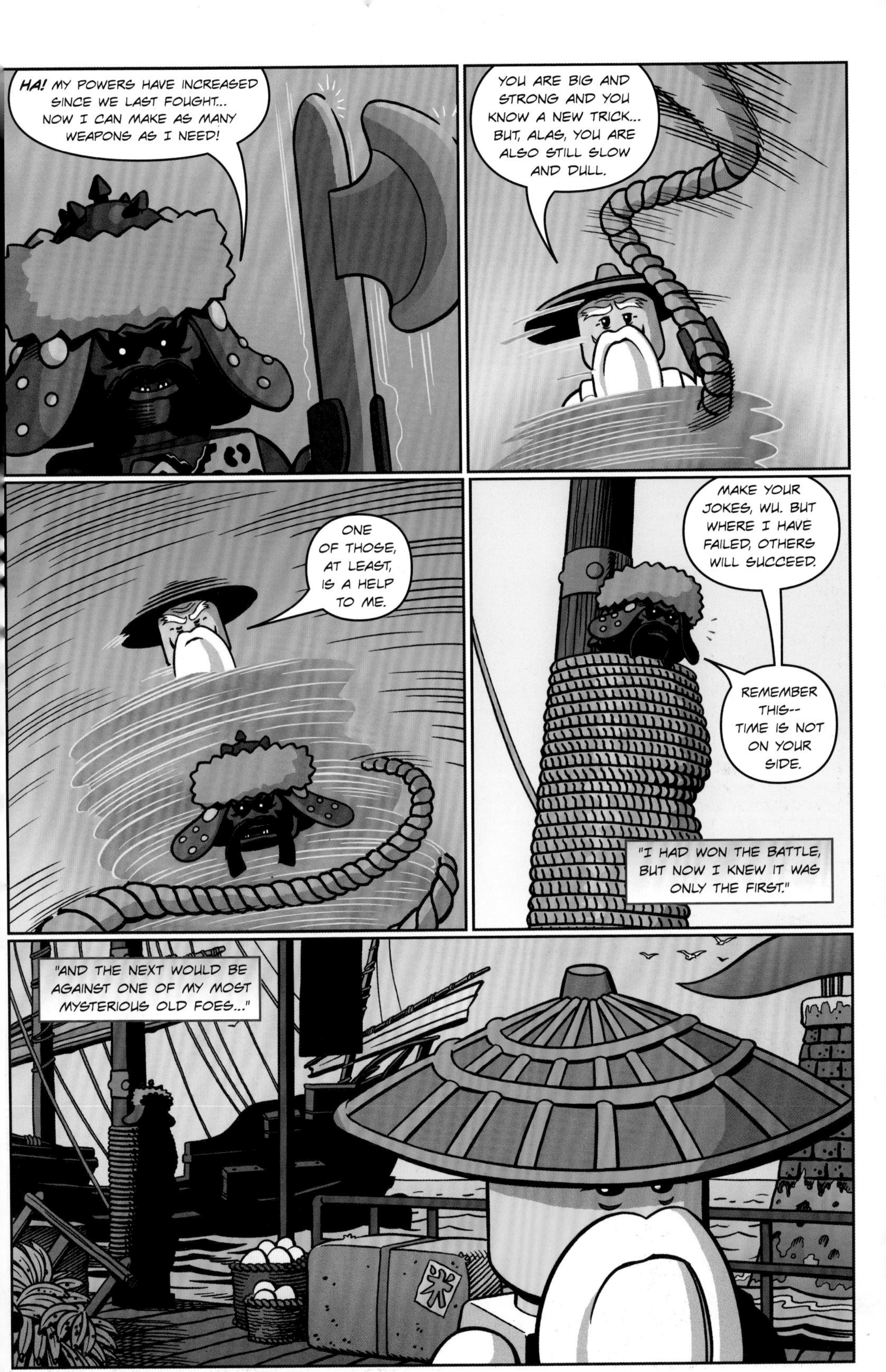
HA! MY POWERS HAVE INCREASED SINCE WE LAST FOUGHT... NOW I CAN MAKE AS MANY WEAPONS AS I NEED!
YOU ARE BIG AND STRONG AND YOU KNOW A NEW TRICK... BUT, ALAS, YOU ARE ALSO STILL SLOW AND DULL.
ONE OF THOSE, AT LEAST, IS A HELP TO ME.
MAKE YOUR JOKES, WU. BUT WHERE I HAVE FAILED, OTHERS WILL SUCCEED.
REMEMBER THIS-- TIME IS NOT ON YOUR SIDE.
"I HAD WON THE BATTLE, BUT NOW I KNEW IT WAS ONLY THE FIRST."
"AND THE NEXT WOULD BE AGAINST ONE OF MY MOST MYSTERIOUS OLD FOES..."

"LONG AGO, AN UNNAMED THIEF DARED TO EXPOSE HIMSELF TO THE POWER OF THE CRONO CRATER, HOPING IT WOULD MAKE HIM IMMORTAL."
"INSTEAD, HE NOW LIVES HIS LIFE ONE SECOND AHEAD OF EVERYONE ELSE..."
"AND HAS BECOME THE TIME NINJA!"
"HE KNOWS WHAT YOU WILL SAY BEFORE YOU SAY IT... AND KNOWS HOW YOU WILL STRIKE BEFORE YOU DO IT."
"I HAD BARELY FOUGHT HIM TO A STANDSTILL WHEN LAST WE MET..."
THERE IS ONLY ONE WAY TO BEAT HIM... BUT CAN I SET MY TRAP IN TIME?
"HOURS LATER, I STOOD IN THE MIDDLE OF THE DESERT OF SHADOW, WAITING FOR MY ENEMY TO ARRIVE."

"HE DID NOT DISAPPOINT ME."
YOU WERE A **FOOL**, SENSEI, TO LET ME KNOW WHERE YOU COULD BE FOUND!
YOU HAVE ONLY MADE IT EASIER FOR ME TO DEFEAT YOU.

OR PERHAPS I MADE IT EASIER FOR YOU TO RUSH TO YOUR DESTRUCTION.

I KNEW YOU WOULD SAY THAT. JUST AS I KNOW WHAT YOU WILL SAY NEXT.
THEN I WILL NOT BOTHER SAYING IT. I WILL JUST ACT.

DIDN'T YOU LEARN THE LAST TIME?

YOU CAN'T HIT A MAN WHO CAN SEE YOUR MOVES BEFORE YOU MAKE THEM.

ACTUALLY, I LEARNED MY LESSONS WELL.

OH, NO...
I CAN SEE WHAT HAPPENS NEXT! I MUST GET AWAY FROM HERE!
ALAS, THOUGH YOU LIVE MOMENTS EARLIER THAN ANYONE ELSE, YOU CAN STILL BE... TOO LATE.
I KNEW YOU WOULD 'SEE' ANY TRAP I SPRUNG BEFORE IT HAPPENED, SO I SET A TRAP YOU WOULD NEED MORE THAN ONE SECOND TO ESCAPE FROM.

YOU MADE ONE MISTAKE, SENSEI-- YOU ARE NOW TRAPPED IN HERE WITH ME.

YOUR POWER LETS YOU DO MANY AMAZING THINGS, TIME NINJA...

UNFORTUNATELY, FLYING IS NOT ONE OF THEM.

YOU SHOULD BE VERY AFRAID, SENSEI. I WOULD BE, IF I WERE YOU... IT WOULD BE THE THING TO DO.

"I WAS SURE THAT WHAT THE TIME NINJA HAD SHOUTED WAS SOME CLUE TO THE IDENTITY OF MY NEXT OPPONENT, BUT I WAS GROWING TIRED AND COULD NOT FIGURE IT OUT."

"I RETURNED TO MY DOJO, FOR I KNEW BOTH MY MIND AND BODY NEEDED REST FOR THE BATTLES TO COME."

"I WASN'T GOING TO GET IT."
HISSSSSS

HISSSSSS
"SOME DARK FORCE HAD ANIMATED MY STAFF... AND IT WAS STRONGER THAN ME!"

"AND IT WASN'T JUST THE STAFF."

"I HAD TO STOP THE SOURCE OF THIS ATTACK, BUT HOW TO FIND IT?"
BOP

"I DIDN'T HAVE TO WORRY. HE FOUND ME."
BAM

CARDINSTO!
WE MEET AGAIN, OLD FOE.

WITH MY POWER OVER NATURE, I CAN COMMAND THE WOOD OF THE FOREST TO TURN AGAINST YOU. GIVEN TIME, YOU COULD PROBABLY DEFEAT YOUR STAFF, EVEN YOUR FURNITURE...

BUT EVEN IF YOUR POWERS WERE AS NUMEROUS AS THE INSECTS IN THE FIELDS, YOU COULD NOT WIN...

YOU SEE, YOUR DOJO IS MADE OF WOOD, TOO.
CRASH

"IT MIGHT HAVE BEEN HOURS OR DAYS BEFORE I MANAGED TO CRAWL OUT FROM THE WRECKAGE OF MY HOME."

"CARDINSTO THE WIZARD WAS LONG GONE, OF COURSE. BUT THAT WASN'T WHAT BOTHERED ME THE MOST."

"SOMEONE WAS DIRECTING THESE ATTACKS, TRYING TO... DESTROY ME? NO, MORE LIKE EXHAUST ME, MAKE ME WEAK."

"I WOULD HAVE TO DEAL WITH THAT ONCE I HAD FINISHED OFF CARDINSTO, WHO WAS BUSY WITH HIS USUAL HOBBY: WORLD CONQUEST."
GO, MY ARMY, DESTROY THE TOWN!

TOGETHER, WE WILL RULE NINJAGO! TOGETHER, WE WILL--
WHAM
FALL, TRICKSTER!

YOU STILL LIVE? I AM IMPRESSED.
BUT ONLY A FOOL WOULD CHALLENGE ME HERE, SURROUNDED BY THE NATURE I COMMAND!

I KNOW ALL ABOUT YOUR POWER, WIZARD...
BUT DO YOU KNOW MINE?

BEHOLD!
BEHOLD WHAT? YOU'RE DIGGING A HOLE.

AND ANOTHER...

I GET IT. YOU DIG WELL.

AND DEEP, MY FOE... DOWN TO WHERE THE THINGS THAT WERE ANCIENT WHEN THIS WORLD WAS NEW STILL DWELL.
YIII! WHAT HAVE YOU DONE?
THE BEAST WANTED TO KNOW WHO DARED TO AWAKEN HIM. I GAVE HIM YOUR NAME.

NO!
MY POWER CAN CONTROL THIS... WHATEVER IT IS!

NO EFFECT! HOW CAN THIS BE?
THIS CREATURE EXISTED BEFORE WHAT WE KNOW OF AS THE NATURAL WORLD.
IT IS NOT A PART OF NATURE, SO YOU HAVE NO POWER OVER IT.

SAVE ME! SAVE ME! I DIDN'T MEAN TO KNOCK YOUR HOUSE DOWN, REALLY!

THEN LET'S TALK ABOUT WHO TOLD YOU TO DESTROY MY DOJO.
YOU-- YOU GOT ME!
BUT WHAT ABOUT THAT MONSTER?

OH, I NEGLECTED TO TELL YOU...
WHOMP
THIS PARTICULAR CREATURE CAN ONLY STAY AWAKE FOR 60 SECONDS AT A TIME.

KEEP AWAY FROM ME!
I AM NOT GOING TO HARM YOU... JUST TAKE YOU FOR A SPIN!

WHOA! STOP!
I'LL TALK!
I'LL TALK!

THEN ANSWER THIS-- WHO IS BEHIND THESE ATTACKS ON ME?
WHO DESTROYED YOUR PRISON?
I'LL TELL YOU, ONCE THE WORLD STOPS WHIRLING AROUND...

IT'S SOMEONE WHO HATES YOU EVEN MORE THAN I DO.
HE'S NOT GOING TO QUIT UNTIL YOU'RE ANCIENT HISTORY, WU.

WHO IS IT? GIVE ME A NAME!
HIS NAME IS--

"SUDDENLY, THERE WAS A BRIGHT FLASH OF LIGHT, BLINDING ME. I COULD HEAR CARDINSTO'S CRIES, BUT COULD NOT SEE HIM."
NO! HELP!

"WHEN THE LIGHT FADED, MY OLD FOE WAS GONE. ALL THAT WAS LEFT WERE--"
SWORDS... AXES... AND BONES? NONE OF THIS MAKES ANY SENSE!

"NOW I WAS TIRED AND MORE CONFUSED THAN EVER. ALL I WANTED WAS TO GO HOME AND REST."

"I HAD FORGOTTEN THAT MY HOME HAD BEEN WRECKED."

"THAT NIGHT, I LAY UNDER THE STARS, TRYING TO SLEEP AND LOST IN MY OWN THOUGHTS."

"I HAD FOUGHT AND BEATEN ALL OF MY OLD FOES INDIVIDUALLY, BUT NEVER ONE AFTER THE OTHER LIKE THIS."
"SOMEONE WAS TRYING TO WEAR ME DOWN... AND SUCCEEDING."

"MORE, EACH VILLAIN KNEW WHO THE NEXT TO FIGHT ME WOULD BE. KIRCHONN TALKED ABOUT TIME..."
BUZZ
"THE TIME NINJA KEPT USING THE WORD 'WOULD,' TO HINT AT THE 'WOOD' CARDINSTO WOULD USE AGAINST ME..."
"AND THE WIZARD?"

"THEN I REMEMBERED-- 'EVEN IF YOUR POWERS WERE AS NUMEROUS AS THE INSECTS IN THE FIELD.' INSECTS!"
BUZZ
BUZZ

"I TURNED TO SEE A MONSTROUS SWARM OF BEES PURSUING ME. THERE WAS ONLY ONE HOPE OF ESCAPE."
BUZZ
BUZZ
BUZZ
BUZZ

"I RAN AS FAST AS I COULD FOR THE NEARBY RIVER."

"IT NEVER OCCURRED TO ME THAT ONE ENEMY MIGHT BE ALLIED WITH ANOTHER, FOR A JOINT ATTACK."

"TWO ENEMIES FELL BEFORE ONE BLOW."
KER-SPLASH

"EVEN FOR A SPINJITZU MASTER, TOO MUCH USE OF ITS POWER CAN BE DRAINING."

"AT LAST, I COULD NO LONGER STAY AWAKE AND I FELL ASLEEP BY THE RIVER."

"I SHOULD HAVE EXPECTED A BAD DREAM."
WHERE AM I? WHAT IS THIS PLACE?
YOU'RE WHERE YOU'RE SUPPOSED TO BE, OLD MAN.

IF YOU THOUGHT YOU COULD BEAT ALL YOUR OLD ENEMIES ON YOUR OWN, YOU WERE DREAMING
SO YOU MIGHT AS WELL BE IN THE DREAM WORLD WITH ME.

WHY WOULD YOU BE LIVING HERE, FIRE DRAGON?
HEY, SOMEONE IS ALWAYS DREAMING ABOUT ME.
I'M COOL AND HOT AT THE SAME TIME, RIGHT?

YOU'LL LIKE IT HERE.
THERE ARE SO MANY THINGS YOU CAN DO!

YOU CAN LIE AROUND AND ENJOY THE SUNSHINE, WITH NO WORRIES.
WOULD YOU LIKE SOME ICED TEA?

YOU CAN RIDE ON RAGING RIVERS...
OR RAGE ON RIDING RIVERS...
WHATEVER FLOATS YOUR CANOE.

OR, IF YOU CAN'T BE HAPPY WITHOUT FIGHTING, WE CAN FIND SOMEBODY FOR YOU TO FIGHT...
A LOT OF SOMEBODIES, IN FACT.

AND ALL YOU HAVE TO DO... IS STAY.
STAY?

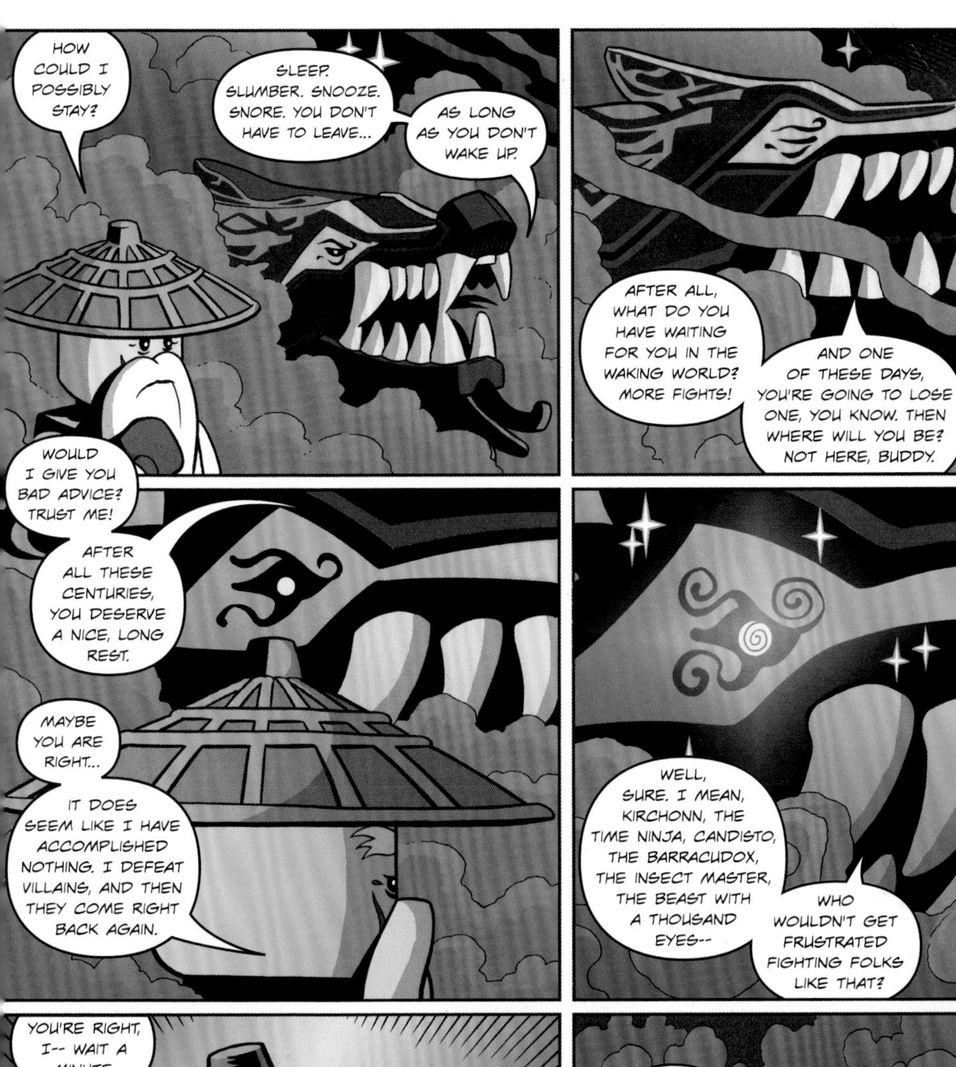
HOW COULD I POSSIBLY STAY?
SLEEP. SLUMBER. SNOOZE. SNORE. YOU DON'T HAVE TO LEAVE...
AS LONG AS YOU DON'T WAKE UP.
AFTER ALL, WHAT DO YOU HAVE WAITING FOR YOU IN THE WAKING WORLD? MORE FIGHTS!
AND ONE OF THESE DAYS, YOU'RE GOING TO LOSE ONE, YOU KNOW. THEN WHERE WILL YOU BE? NOT HERE, BUDDY.
WOULD I GIVE YOU BAD ADVICE? TRUST ME!
AFTER ALL THESE CENTURIES, YOU DESERVE A NICE, LONG REST.
MAYBE YOU ARE RIGHT...
IT DOES SEEM LIKE I HAVE ACCOMPLISHED NOTHING. I DEFEAT VILLAINS, AND THEN THEY COME RIGHT BACK AGAIN.
WELL, SURE. I MEAN, KIRCHONN, THE TIME NINJA, CANDISTO, THE BARRACUDOX, THE INSECT MASTER, THE BEAST WITH A THOUSAND EYES--
WHO WOULDN'T GET FRUSTRATED FIGHTING FOLKS LIKE THAT?

YOU'RE RIGHT, I-- WAIT A MINUTE.
I HAVEN'T FOUGHT THE BEAST WITH A THOUSAND EYES IN THE LAST FEW DAYS.

OOPS.

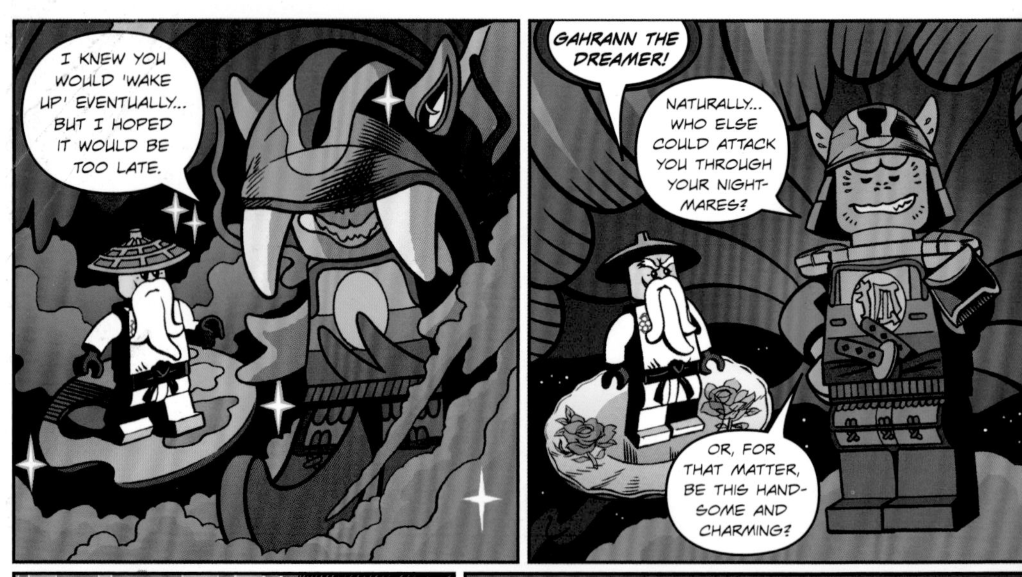
I KNEW YOU WOULD 'WAKE UP' EVENTUALLY... BUT I HOPED IT WOULD BE TOO LATE.
GAHRANN THE DREAMER!
NATURALLY... WHO ELSE COULD ATTACK YOU THROUGH YOUR NIGHT-MARES?
OR, FOR THAT MATTER, BE THIS HAND-SOME AND CHARMING?

NOW THAT I KNOW IT IS YOU, I CAN ARM MY DREAM SELF. PREPARE FOR BATTLE!
SILLY MORTAL, THAT'S NOT A STICK...
THIS IS A STICK!

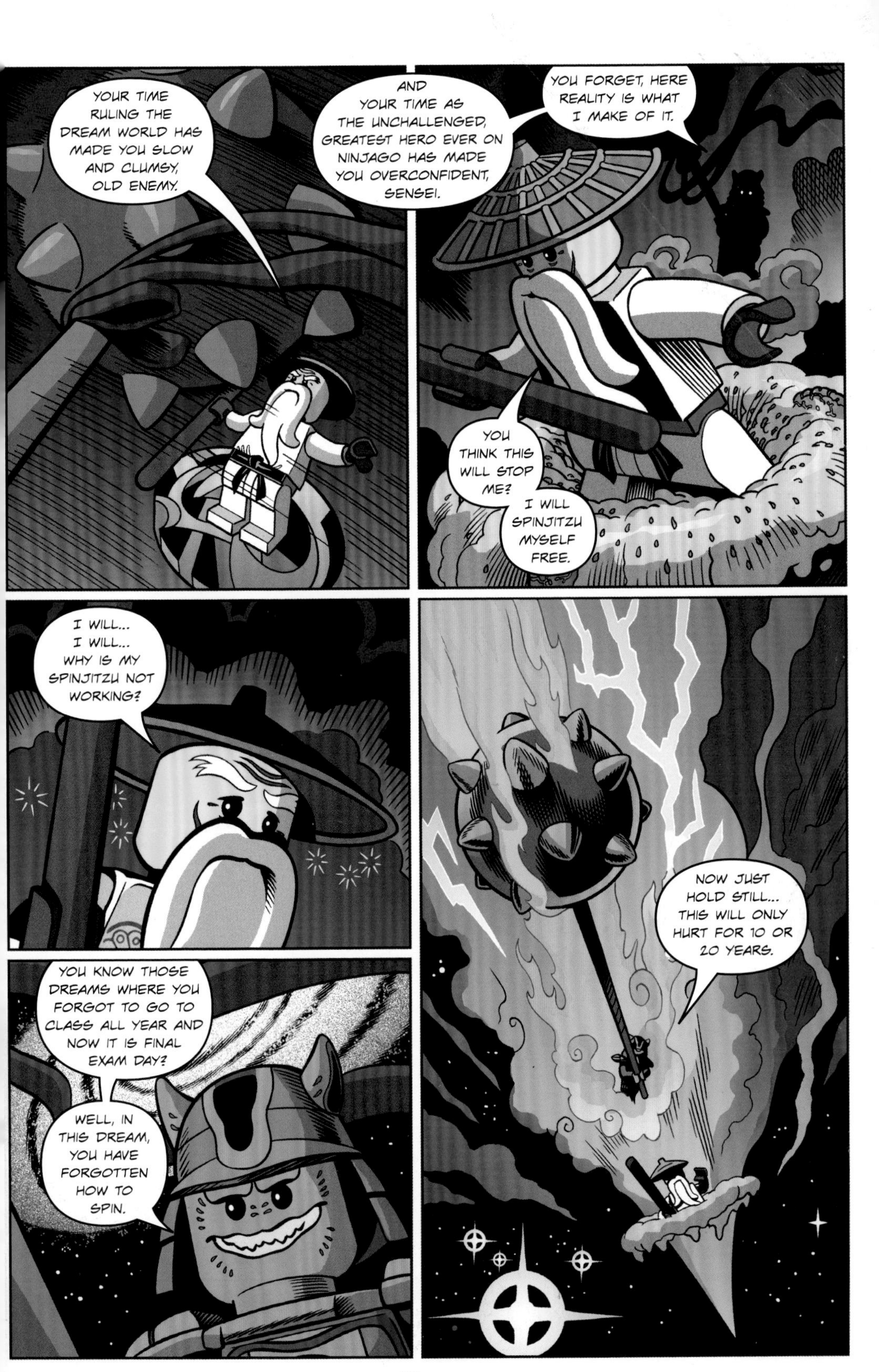
YOUR TIME RULING THE DREAM WORLD HAS MADE YOU SLOW AND CLUMSY, OLD ENEMY.
AND YOUR TIME AS THE UNCHALLENGED, GREATEST HERO EVER ON NINJAGO HAS MADE YOU OVERCONFIDENT, SENSEI.
YOU FORGET, HERE REALITY IS WHAT I MAKE OF IT.
YOU THINK THIS WILL STOP ME?
I WILL SPINJITZU MYSELF FREE.
I WILL... I WILL... WHY IS MY SPINJITZU NOT WORKING?
YOU KNOW THOSE DREAMS WHERE YOU FORGOT TO GO TO CLASS ALL YEAR AND NOW IT IS FINAL EXAM DAY?
WELL, IN THIS DREAM, YOU HAVE FORGOTTEN HOW TO SPIN.
NOW JUST HOLD STILL... THIS WILL ONLY HURT FOR 10 OR 20 YEARS.

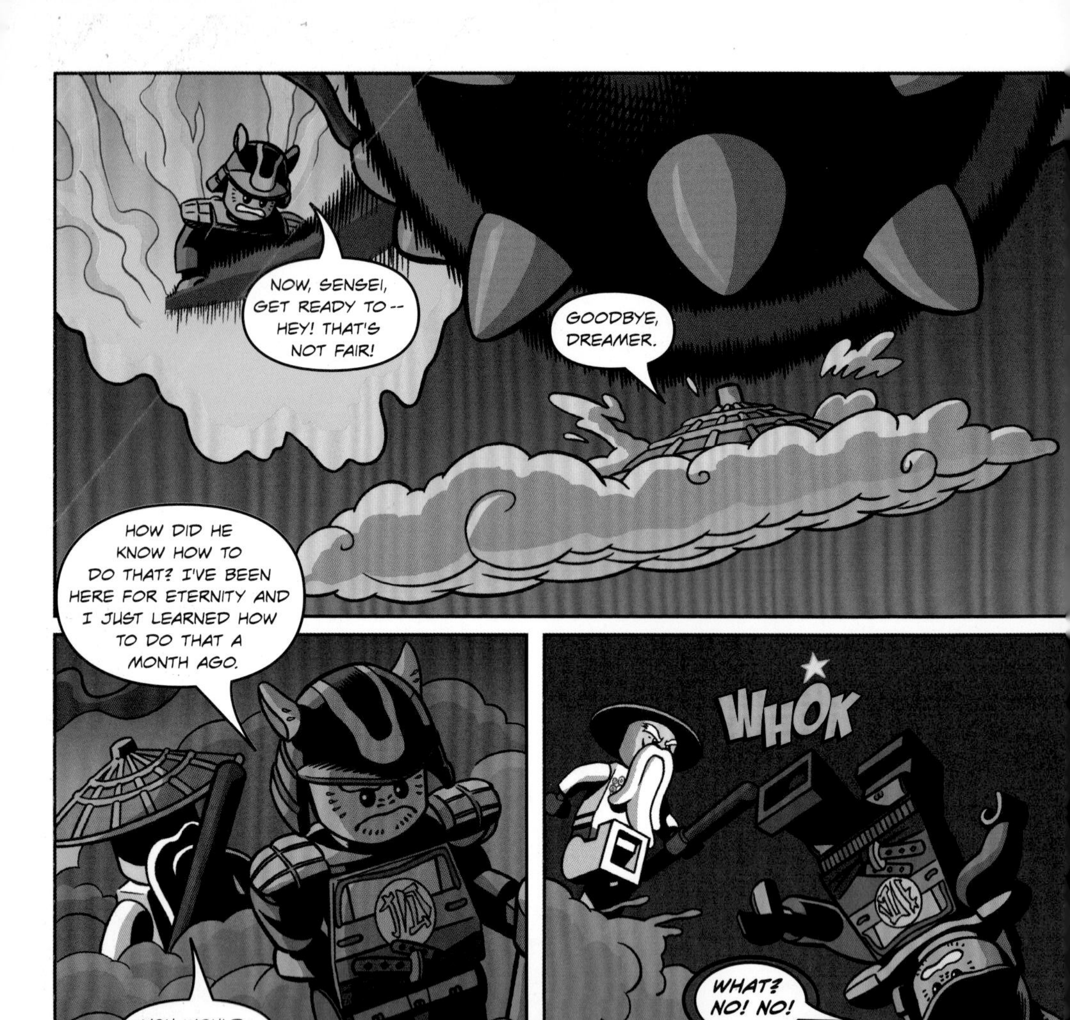
NOW, SENSEI, GET READY TO -- HEY! THAT'S NOT FAIR!
GOODBYE, DREAMER.
HOW DID HE KNOW HOW TO DO THAT? I'VE BEEN HERE FOR ETERNITY AND I JUST LEARNED HOW TO DO THAT A MONTH AGO.
YOU WOULD BE SURPRISED WHAT I KNOW.
WHOK
WHAT? NO! NO!

THAT IS NOT A FATE I WOULD WISH ON ANYONE, BUT HE WHO LIVES BY VIOLENCE--
AAAAHHHHHH!

OH, SENSEI...
WHAT--?!

MADE YOU LOOK!

YOU DIDN'T REALLY THINK IT WOULD BE SO EASY TO BEAT ME, DID YOU?
IN THIS REALM, I AM KING, AFTER ALL.

YES, YOU ARE A POWERFUL KING...
SO WHY DO YOU SERVE ANOTHER?

EH? WHAT ARE YOU TALKING ABOUT?

YOU ARE NOT THE MASTERMIND BEHIND THE OTHER ATTACKS ON ME...
THEY WERE TOO SLOPPY FOR A GENIUS SUCH AS YOURSELF.

I CAN'T ARGUE WITH THAT.
BUT YOU ARE WORKING FOR THE SAME BEING MY OTHER FOES WERE...
SOMEONE POWERFUL ENOUGH TO COMMAND A KING?
WHO WOULD THAT BE?

YOU ARE TRYING TO MAKE ME ANGRY SO THAT I WILL SAY SOMETHING I SHOULDN'T.
SO IS THERE SOMETHING TO SAY?
I DIDN'T SAY THAT.
THEN SAY WHAT IT IS YOU DID SAY.
YOU'RE GIVING ME A HEADACHE...
GOOD THING I ALWAYS CARRY A SPARE. NOW, WHERE WERE YOU? OH, THAT'S RIGHT...
YOU'RE MY PRISONER FOR ETERNITY.
I DIS- AGREE.
SURRENDER, DREAMER, BEFORE I GET ANGRY.

NO ONE GIVES ME ORDERS!

REALLY?

SOMEONE DOES NOW.
GET OFF ME! WITH YOUR WEIGHT ADDED, WE'LL FALL!
SO? THIS REALM IS ENDLESS. WE CAN FALL, BUT NEVER LAND...
AND IT'S NOT THE FALLING THAT IS USUALLY THE PROBLEM, IT'S THE SUDDEN STOP.
YOU FOOL! DON'T YOU REALIZE WHAT LIES AT THE BOTTOM OF THE DREAM WORLD?
THE DREAMS OF... I ALMOST CAN'T BEAR TO SAY IT... HAPPY PEOPLE.

IT'S ALL RAINBOWS AND PUPPY DOGS DOWN THERE. HORRIBLE! **HORRIBLE!**
THEN WHY NOT JUST BAR THEM FROM YOUR REALM?
I TRIED THAT. BUT HAPPY PEOPLE SLEEP WELL...
SO THEY ARE **ALWAYS** DREAMING.
NOW I'LL HAVE TO DO SOMETHING I REALLY HATE DOING.
I ALWAYS SPRAIN SOME-THING DOING THIS...

WELL, I GUESS IF YOU HAVE TO DREAM, **DREAM BIG.**

THAT WAS CLOSE. YOU KNOW, IN THE WAKING WORLD, YOU'RE A HERO, SENSEI...
BUT IN THE DREAM WORLD, YOU ARE A COLOSSAL PAIN IN THE NECK.
I DO MY BEST.

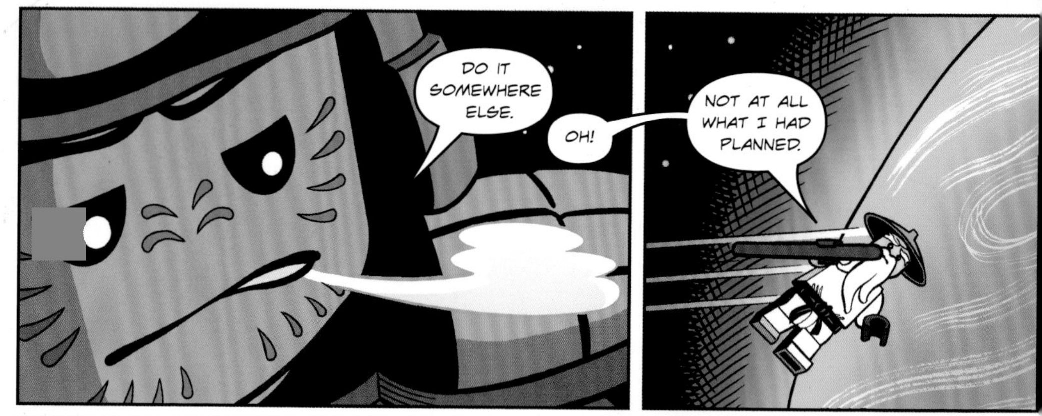
DO IT SOMEWHERE ELSE.
OH!
NOT AT ALL WHAT I HAD PLANNED.

SPLASH

I NEED TO INVEST IN WATERPROOF ROBES.
HERE, LET ME HELP YOU.

GARMADON!
WHAT'S THE MATTER? YOU ACT LIKE YOU NEVER SAW ME BEFORE.

I HAVEN'T... NOT FOR A LONG TIME.
WE JUST HAD BREAKFAST TWO HOURS AGO!
ANYWAY, LOOK WHAT I FOUND IN THE GARDEN... TRIED TO BITE ME, THE UGLY THING!
YOU MEAN... IT DIDN'T BITE YOU?
NAH, IT TRIED TO, BUT I WAS TOO FAST FOR IT. SO WHAT DO YOU WANT TO DO TODAY?
THIS IS INSANE. THAT SNAKE WILL ONE DAY GROW TO BE THE GREAT DEVOURER...
THOUGH NOT BEFORE IT BITES MY BROTHER AND CORRUPTS HIM. BUT IF HE WASN'T BITTEN, THEN HE WILL NEVER TURN EVIL.
HEY, NINJAGO TO WU-- ARE YOU OKAY? I MEAN, YOU LOOK... OLD.

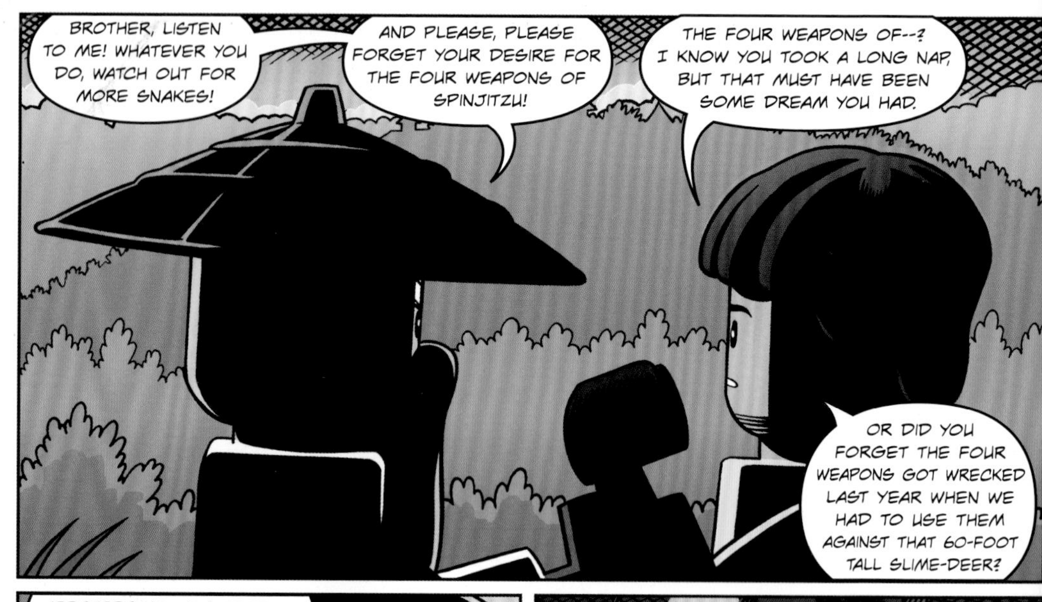

BROTHER, LISTEN TO ME! WHATEVER YOU DO, WATCH OUT FOR MORE SNAKES!
AND PLEASE, PLEASE FORGET YOUR DESIRE FOR THE FOUR WEAPONS OF SPINJITZU!
THE FOUR WEAPONS OF--? I KNOW YOU TOOK A LONG NAP, BUT THAT MUST HAVE BEEN SOME DREAM YOU HAD.
OR DID YOU FORGET THE FOUR WEAPONS GOT WRECKED LAST YEAR WHEN WE HAD TO USE THEM AGAINST THAT 60-FOOT TALL SLIME-DEER?

WRECKED? NO, YOU TRIED TO STEAL THEM AND WOUND UP IN THE UNDERWORLD AND... AND... I'M NOT MAKING SENSE TO YOU, AM I?
NOT MUCH; NO. MAYBE YOU SHOULD HAVE SOME TEA.

THIS CAN'T BE REAL... BUT WHAT IF IT IS? WHAT IF I TOOK A NAP AND SIMPLY DREAMT ALL THAT HAPPENED AGAINST MY FOES?
WHAT IF GARMADON IS SAFE AND WELL AND HE AND I ARE STILL TRUE BROTHERS?

IF YOU'RE DONE DAYDREAMING, THE GUARDS BROUGHT IN FOUR TROUBLEMAKERS AND WE NEED TO DECIDE THEIR PUNISHMENT.
HMMM? OH, YES, COMING...

I REALLY DON'T KNOW WHAT THE PROBLEM IS WITH YOUNG PEOPLE TODAY. THEY HAVE ALL THE ADVANTAGES, AND ALL THEY WANT TO DO IS SPIN AROUND ALL DAY.
SPIN AROUND?

THAT'S WHAT I SAID.
MAYBE I'M NOT DOING IT FAST ENOUGH.
WHOA! MAKE THE ROOM STOP SPINNING!
WHY DID WE THINK THIS WAS A GOOD IDEA?

"SOMEHOW, I SEEMED TO KNOW MUCH OF WHAT WOULD HAPPEN IN THE FUTURE... OR WAS SUPPOSED TO HAPPEN. AND, THOUGH I HAD YET TO MEET ANY OF YOU IN PERSON, I ALREADY KNEW OF YOU AND YOUR POTENTIAL. SO YOU CAN IMAGINE MY SHOCK AT SEEING THE FOUR OF YOU ASSEMBLED."
WAIT A MINUTE, BUT THEY'RE... AND YOU'RE... YOU'RE--

--GAHRANN!
OOOF!

I HAD YOU GOING THERE FOR A MINUTE, ADMIT IT! BUT IN THE END, YOU JUST AREN'T ANY FUN AT ALL... EVEN IN YOUR DREAMS, THOSE NINJA HAD TO SHOW UP.

SO I AM GOING TO SAY SOMETHING I HAVE NEVER SAID TO ANYONE...

WAKE UP!

"AND WAKE UP I DID, WITH THE MEMORY OF THAT CRUEL TRICK GAHRANN THE DREAMER HAD PLAYED ON ME."

"I HAD HAD ENOUGH."

KRASH
"NO LONGER WOULD I WAIT FOR MY ENEMIES TO ATTACK ME. I WOULD TAKE THE BATTLE TO THEM."

"I WOULD STOP THEM BEFORE THEY COULD HOPE TO STOP ME."

"ACROSS THE WORLD I TRAVELLED, FROM THE FROZEN NORTH..."
"TO THE BURNING DESERTS..."
"AND EVEN BENEATH THE PLANET ITSELF, TO THE LAIR OF THE LIVING DIAMONDS."
"FOR WEEKS AND MONTHS, I BATTLED, CRUSHING THE DARK FORCES WHEREVER I FOUND THEM. I THOUGHT I HAD WON A GREAT VICTORY."
"IN ONE OF MY FINAL BATTLES, I CHALLENGED THE POWERFUL MASK OF MALICE."
WITH YOUR DEFEAT, I WILL HAVE DEFEATED ALL THAT IS EVIL IN THIS WORLD!
REALLY?

IS THAT WHAT YOU THINK?
IF I COULD LAUGH, I WOULD.
KA-THOOM
TELL ME-- YOU ARE THE GREATEST HERO ON NINJAGO, AREN'T YOU?
I AM THE ONLY HERO ON NINJAGO.
AND YOU WIN EVERY FIGHT, DON'T YOU? NO ONE CAN DEFEAT YOU?
TRY ME, AND SEE!

HERE. I'LL STOP FLYING. TAKE YOUR SHOT. IT WON'T DO YOU ANY GOOD.

WHAT... ARE YOU TALKING ABOUT?
THAT'S BETTER.
YOU FIGURED OUT THOSE OTHER LOSERS WERE JUST TRYING TO TIRE YOU OUT, RIGHT?
OF COURSE.

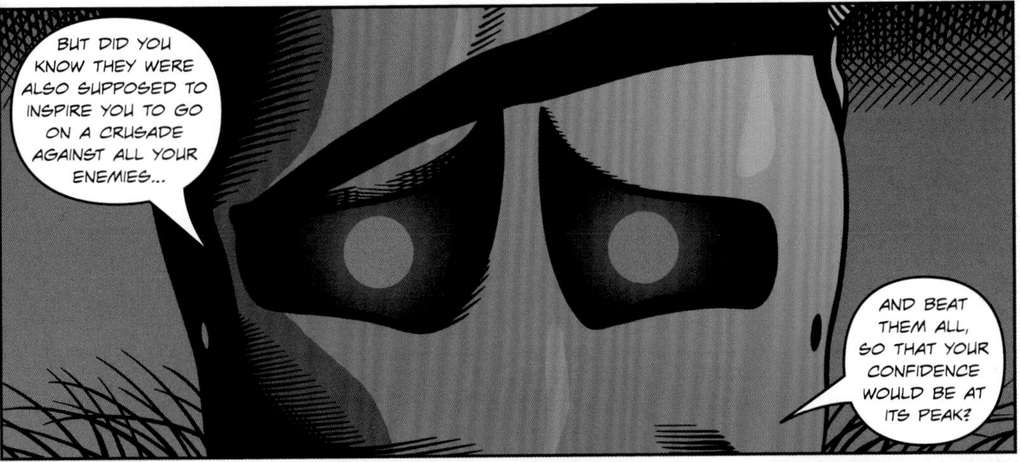
BUT DID YOU KNOW THEY WERE ALSO SUPPOSED TO INSPIRE YOU TO GO ON A CRUSADE AGAINST ALL YOUR ENEMIES...
AND BEAT THEM ALL, SO THAT YOUR CONFIDENCE WOULD BE AT ITS PEAK?

I WOULD BECOME CONVINCED OF MY POWER, AND THEN...
YOU GOT IT. THEN, **WHAP**!

YOU WANT TO SEE YOUR REAL ENEMY, SENSEI? LOOK IN THE MIRROR.

"I SAT AND THOUGHT FOR A LONG TIME ABOUT WHAT THE MASK HAD SAID. 'LOOK IN THE MIRROR... IN THE MIRROR...'"

"AND THEN I KNEW."
A MIRROR? OH, NO...

"I RUSHED TO THE NEAREST VILLAGE..."
A MIRROR! MY FRIENDS, PLEASE, SOMEONE GIVE ME A MIRROR.

I FOUND ONE, FINALLY, IN THE WINDOW OF AN ANTIQUE SHOP, AND WHEN I LOOKED INSIDE..."

"I KNEW WHAT I WOULD SEE."

"GARMADON!"
HELLO, BROTHER. HOW NICE TO SEE YOU.

YOU ARE NO BROTHER OF MINE, DARK ONE!
I REALISED, WHEN THE MASK OF MALICE SPOKE OF A MIRROR, THAT YOU MUST BE THE ONE BEHIND ALL THIS!

OF COURSE YOU DID.
FOR WE BOTH KNOW THAT MIRRORS ARE WINDOWS INTO THE UNDERWORLD, WHERE YOU EXILED ME SO LONG AGO.
BUT LET ME GET A BIT MORE COMFORT-ABLE...

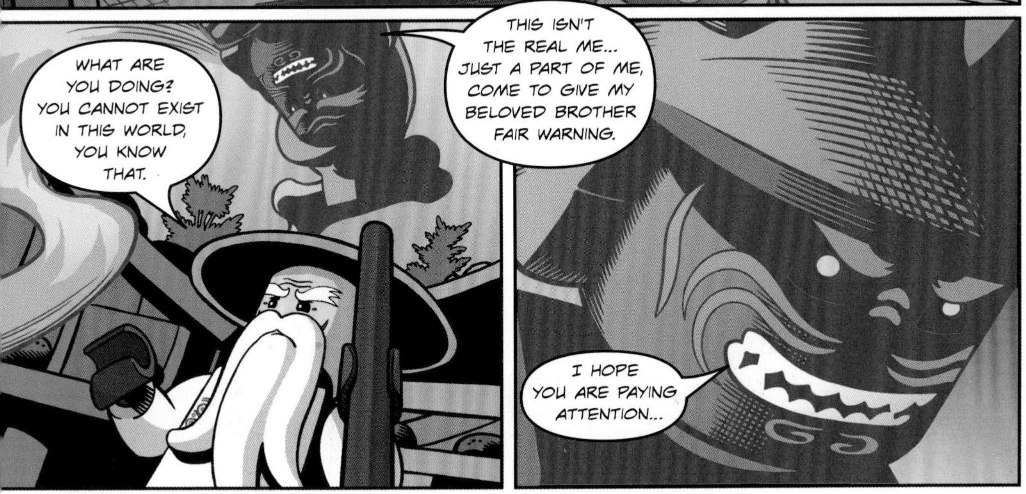
WHAT ARE YOU DOING? YOU CANNOT EXIST IN THIS WORLD, YOU KNOW THAT.
THIS ISN'T THE REAL ME... JUST A PART OF ME, COME TO GIVE MY BELOVED BROTHER FAIR WARNING.
I HOPE YOU ARE PAYING ATTENTION...

YOU KNOW HOW I HATE TO BE **IGNORED!**

VERY IMPRESSIVE. STAY UP THERE, PERHAPS THE VILLAGERS CAN USE YOU AS A FLOAT IN THE NEXT PARADE.
YOUR HUMOUR, LIKE YOUR CAUSE, IS HOPE-LESS.
I AM RETURNING, BROTHER, TO TAKE WHAT IS MINE-- AND YOU WON'T STOP ME.
AND ALL OF THIS--
THE DESTRUCTION OF THE PRISON, THE ENDLESS FIGHTS--
THAT WAS YOUR WAY OF SAYING HELLO?
AT FIRST, I HOPED TO WEAR YOU DOWN BEFORE MY ARRIVAL...
THEN, I DECIDED TO MAKE YOU SO OVERCONFIDENT YOU WOULD NEVER SEE ME COMING. NOW?
I THINK I WILL JUST ELIMINATE YOU AS A THREAT.
TELL ME, BROTHER, HOW WILL YOU KNOW WHICH ONE OF US TO FIGHT?
I DON'T NEED TO TRY TO SOLVE THAT QUESTION.

NOT WHEN I CAN BLOW ALL OF YOU AWAY!
AS I SUSPECTED... ALL ILLUSIONS.
TRAPPED IN THE UNDERWORLD, GARMADON CANNOT RETURN TO NINJAGO...
EVEN HE WOULDN'T DARE TO TAKE THE RISKS THAT WOULD INVOLVE.
TO HAVE MY REVENGE, I WILL DARE ANYTHING, WU.
THEN I WILL STOP YOU AGAIN, VILLAIN, AS I DID THE LAST TIME!
NO EFFECT!
HA HA HA!
COOL OFF, BROTHER!
UNNNGHH
SPLOOSH

SHOW YOURSELF, BROTHER --YOUR REAL SELF-- AND FIGHT WITH HONOR.

OH, TOO MUCH OF ME IS STILL IN THE UNDERWORLD FOR THAT...
...AND BESIDES, I HAVE NO HONOUR.

"GARMADON HAD DISSOLVED INTO THE MIRROR..."
BUT NOW YOU KNOW I AM COMING.

"...AND THE MIRROR BEGAN TO CRACK..."
YOU JUST DON'T KNOW WHEN OR WHERE.

"FINALLY, THE MIRROR SHATTERED!"
CRASH

"USING ALL MY SKILLS I WAS ABLE TO DODGE THE SHARDS OF GLASS..."

"GARMADON WAS GONE, LEAVING ONLY THE SHATTERED MIRROR GLASS BEHIND HIM. BUT I WAS DETERMINED NOT TO LET IT END THERE."

"THAT MIRROR HAD BEEN TOUCHED BY HIS POWER. IF I RESTORED IT, PERHAPS I COULD FIND HIM AGAIN."

"WHEN AT LAST I WAS DONE, I DARED TO LOOK INSIDE..."

"AND I SAW... THE FUTURE... A FUTURE FILLED WITH SOME OF THE GREATEST MENACES I COULD IMAGINE."

THAT WAS WHEN I REALISED... I COULD NO LONGER AFFORD TO FIGHT ALONE.

THE REST YOU KNOW. I RECRUITED AND TRAINED THE FOUR OF YOU FOR THE FIGHT AGAINST GARMADON, AND THE OTHER FOES I SAW IN THAT BROKEN MIRROR.
WELL, WE DON'T KNOW EVERY-THING.

KAI'S RIGHT-- YOU SAW THE FUTURE!
TELL ME, WILL I BE FAMOUS AS THE WORLD'S GREATEST INVENTOR... OR THE WORLD'S GREATEST NINJA?

I THINK THERE ARE MORE IMPORTANT QUESTIONS TO ASK...
LIKE, DID THE SENSEI SEE ANY THREATS BEYOND THE STONE WARRIORS?

IT IS NOT GOOD FOR ANY MAN TO KNOW HIS FUTURE, COLE...
BELIEVE ME, I KNOW. BUT YOU SEEM TO BE MISSING THE POINT OF MY TALE...

EACH OF YOU TRIED TO CHALLENGE THE STONE WARRIORS ALONE, AND LOST.
BUT YOU WERE MEANT TO BE A TEAM. THERE IS NO SHAME IN ADMITTING YOU NEED HELP.

WAS THAT THE POINT? I THOUGHT IT WAS THAT GARMADON IS A REAL--
JAY!
YOU SEEMED TO DO PRETTY WELL ON YOUR OWN, SENSEI.
INDEED. YOU WON ALL THE FIGHTS.

PERHAPS I TOLD IT WRONG...
PERHAPS MY TEAMMATES WOULDN'T GET THE POINT OF A STORY IF THEY SAT ON IT.
AT LEAST IT'S GOOD TO KNOW ALL YOUR OLD ENEMIES ARE WHERE THEY CAN'T HURT ANYONE. RIGHT?

ONE CAN ONLY HOPE.

HEY, IF ANY OF THOSE GUYS SHOW UP, WE'LL POUND THEM... AS A TEAM!
ONE CHALLENGE AT A TIME, JAY, PLEASE? STONE WARRIORS FIRST, EVERYONE ELSE LATER.
COME ON, ZANE, WHERE'S YOUR SENSE OF ADVENTURE?
NEVER THE END.

SNEAK PEEK

It has been a month since the defeat of the Stone Warriors. Peace has returned to the world of Ninjago...

But the Ninja know they must keep training, just in case trouble strikes again...
NOW, JAY, I'LL--
HA! KAI, DID YOU EXPECT ME TO WAIT FOR IT?

LET'S SEE HOW YOU LIKE THE PYTHON THROW, AND-- OOF!... COME ON-- WHY ISN'T THIS WORKING?
MAYBE YOU'RE DOING IT WRONG?

THEY HAVE ACCOMPLISHED MUCH, MY NINJA... BUT THEY STILL HAVE MUCH TO LEARN.
WELL, THEY HAVE AN EXCELLENT TEACHER, MY BROTHER.

PERHAPS I HAVE TAUGHT THEM ALL I KNOW. THEY WOULD BENEFIT FROM A NEW INSTRUCTOR.
ME? WHAT COULD I TEACH THEM, OTHER THAN HOW TO BRING MISERY?

DESTINY OF DOOM

Greg Farshtey – Worrisome Writer
Jolyon Yates – Anxious Artist
Laurie E. Smith – Cautious Colourist
Bryan Senka – Leery Letterer
Michael Petranek – Apprehensive Associate Editor
Jim Salicrup – Expectant Editor-in-Chief

YES, YOU WERE A DESTROYER, ONCE...
NOW YOU HAVE THE CHANCE TO BE A BUILDER. THE CHOICE IS YOURS.
I TRY AND TRY AND I JUST CAN'T MASTER THAT MOVE!
THERE MUST BE SOME SIMPLE TRICK I AM MISSING.
THERE IS. YOU HAVE TO DROP YOUR RIGHT SHOULDER AS YOU MOVE IN SO YOU CAN GET THE RIGHT LEVERAGE.

WHO ASKED YOU? IN CASE YOU HAVEN'T NOTICED, WE'RE NOT SKELETONS OR STATUES.
WE'RE NINJA!
I KNOW THAT. I WAS SIMPLY TRY-ING TO--

DON'T. JUST DON'T. AFTER ALL YOU'VE DONE, YOU'RE CRAZY IF YOU THINK WE'LL LISTEN TO YOU!
KAI, COME ON. BACK OFF.

I DON'T BLAME YOU FOR HOW YOU FEEL, KAI.
MAYBE MY BEING HERE AT ALL IS A MISTAKE.

Don't Miss LEGO NINJAGO #8 "Destiny of Doom"!